DNA

ALVIN SILVERSTEIN • VIRGINIA SILVERSTEIN • LAURA SILVERSTEIN NUNN

TWENTY-FIRST CENTURY BOOKS

BROOKFIELD, CONNECTICUT

Cover photograph courtesy of SuperStock
Photographs courtesy of SuperStock: pp. 4, 21, 51 (© Ron Dahlquist); Photo Researchers, Inc.: pp. 6
(© Stephen J. Krasemann), 33 (© Meckes/Ottawa), 34 (© Mike Devlin/SPL), 46 (© Noah Poritz), 50
(© Ken M. Highfill); PhotoEdit: p. 7 (© Mary Kate Denny); © 2001 Dennis Kunkel Microscopy, Inc./Dennis
Kunkel: pp. 11, 20, 22; Peter Arnold, Inc.: pp. 12 (© Leonard Lessin), 23 (© Leonard Lessin); National Library of
Medicine, History of Medicine Collection: p. 25; Visuals Unlimited, Inc.: pp. 31 (© Charles Philip), 41
(© Brad Mogen), 42 (© Inga Spence), 54 (© Inga Spence); AP/Wide World Photos: p. 40

Library of Congress Cataloging-in-Publication Data
Silverstein, Alvin.
DNA / by Alvin & Virginia Silverstein & Laura Silverstein Nunn.
p. cm.
Summary: Explains the structure and function of DNA and discusses current relevant scientific research.
Includes bibliographical references and index.
Contest: The code of life—What is DNA?—How heredity works—When the code goes wrong—The Genome
Project—The DNA detective—Tinkering with DNA.
ISBN 0-7613-2257-4 (lib. bdg.)
1. DNA—Juvenile literature. [1. DNA. 2. Genetics.] I. Silverstein, Virginia B. II. Nunn, Laura Silverstein. III. Title.
QP624 .S55 2002 572.8¢6—dc21 2001043468

Published by Twenty-First Century Books
A Division of The Millbrook Press
2 Old New Milford Rd., Brookfield, Connecticut 06804
www.millbrookpress.com

CONTENTS

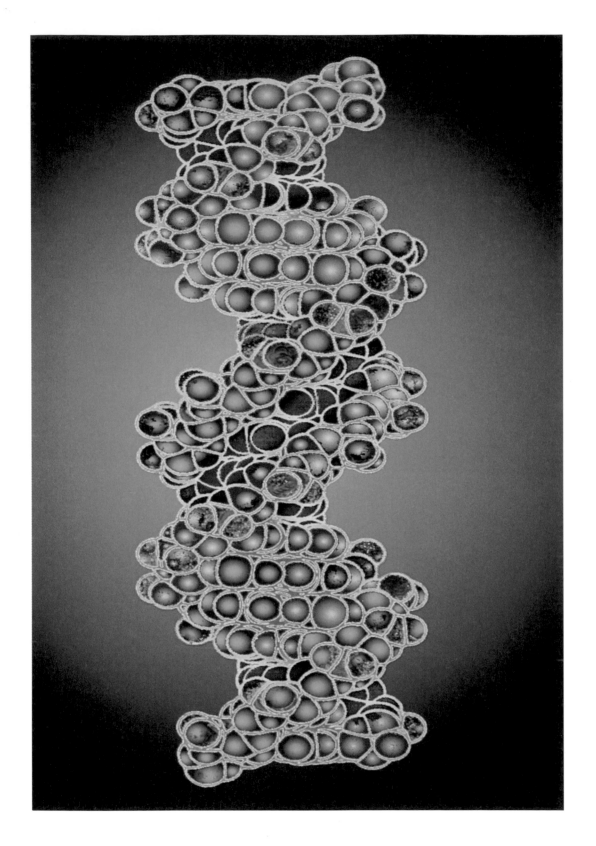

✦ ONE ✦

THE CODE OF LIFE

Why does a dog have puppies and not kittens? Why do a hen's eggs hatch into chicks instead of ducklings? Why does an acorn grow into an oak tree instead of a sunflower? And why does a human give birth to a human baby rather than to a baby horse? All these living things follow the laws of nature.

While the various creatures on Earth may seem different, they all have something in common: Each living thing is made up of tiny units, called **cells**. Cells are the building blocks of life. Just as bricks are stacked to build a wall, cells are the bricks that build a living creature. The larger the organism, the more cells it contains.

So in a sense, all living things—from a tiny ant to a flowering dogwood tree to an enormous whale—share a common thread: the cells that compose them. And yet, there are distinct differences. A mouse looks very different from an elephant, and a spider in no way, shape, or form resembles a giraffe. Even creatures within the same species look different from one another. You would not confuse a Great Dane with a Chihuahua or a dachshund. And you most likely do not look like any of your friends.

> ### DID YOU KNOW?
>
> Your body is made up of trillions of cells. Can you imagine how many cells there are in the largest creature on Earth, the blue whale? It can grow to more than 100 feet (30 meters) long!

What makes this elephant and its newborn so similar, and yet slightly different? The answer lies in the genetic material inside their cells.

✦ YOUR INSTRUCTION MANUAL ✦

If all living things have cells in common, then what makes organisms so different? The key is what's inside the cells: genetic material, called **DNA (deoxyribonucleic acid)**. DNA is the working part of the **chromosomes**, small rodlike structures in cells that contain **genes**, the units of heredity. Genes carry the information that determines the characteristics of a cell and the instructions for making new cells. Many new cells are formed as a baby grows into an adult. New cells are also formed when different parts of the body are damaged and need repair.

The information in DNA is "written" in a special chemical code. Each living thing has a code that is unique to each individual. Scientists have been learning to read the DNA code. They hope to use this knowledge to help treat diseases that are caused by genetic errors. Uncovering the mysteries of DNA has also allowed scientists to trace our ancestry. DNA has even become a useful tool in solving crimes.

What's most interesting about the genetic code is that although the differences from one person to another are enough to make us quite diverse, most of the code is almost exactly the same in all living things—viruses, bacteria, plants, animals, and humans. In fact, the code of life, which holds the secrets to all our differences, also holds the answer to the many ways in which all forms of life are so much alike.

Your genetic code determines how tall you can become, the shape of your face, the color of your hair and eyes, and everything else that makes you unique.

WHAT IS DNA?

Back in the 1800s, before there were telephones, radios, or satellites, people could communicate across great distances by telegraph. Telegraph messages were sent by tapping out a code that involved only two "letters," dot (·) and dash (—). In Morse code (named after Samuel Morse, the inventor of the telegraph), these two signs can spell out any word or sentence in the English language.

The language of DNA is spelled out in a code that is a bit more complicated than Morse code. It uses a four-"letter" chemical alphabet. These chemical letters are combined in a special order to form "words," "sentences," and "paragraphs," all linked together into long DNA chains. The DNA in each cell is like a recipe book, divided into a number of "chapters" (the chromosomes). Within each chapter are a number of individual recipes—the genes, each of which contains the instructions for making a particular product. The same four letters can be combined in many different ways to spell out the many different traits in an organism.

You might expect that genes are lined up along the DNA chain like the beads of a necklace. Actually, though, chromosomes are a lot more complicated than that. Only a small portion of each DNA molecule consists of genes; there are long stretches of base pairs that apparently don't do anything other than take up space. Scientists have labeled these seemingly useless parts **junk DNA**. Some of them are found between genes, like the spacers between the beads on a necklace, but some bits of "junk" are actually inserted into the genes themselves. These inserted pieces, called **introns**, are like the commercial breaks in a TV drama. They interrupt the story, which is told by **exons**—the parts of the gene attached to the introns. When the cell makes working copies of a gene, the introns are snipped out so that only the chain of exons remains, in much the same way you could use the controls of a VCR to edit out the commercials when you are recording a TV show.

What is all that junk DNA doing there? Some scientists believe that not all of it may be as useless as it seems. Some of it may contain controls and switches that influence how the nearby genes work. Some parts seem to be leftovers from long-ago ancestors, "ghost genes" that got changed during evolution so that they no longer contain instructions the cell can read. And some of the junk DNA may serve as raw material for new genes that may be useful in the future.

✦ THE DNA MODEL ✦

You may remember that DNA is short for *deoxyribonucleic acid*. The "nucleic" part of its name comes from the fact that it is found mainly in the **nucleus** of a cell. The nucleus is the cell's control center; it contains the genetically coded instructions for the cell's activities, including growth and reproduction. All these instructions are spelled out in the chromosomes, in the chemical units that make up DNA.

DNA is a long, threadlike chain of chemical units called **nucleotides**, each of which consists of three parts: a phosphate, a sugar (deoxyribose), and a substance called a nitrogen base. The sugar phosphates link together to form a chain (they are the backbone of the chain), and the nitrogen bases stick out and can react with other bases on a different chain. So DNA is actually a double chain, consisting of two long strings (strands) of nucleotides linked together by chemical bonds between nitrogen bases. The DNA molecule is curled in a spi-

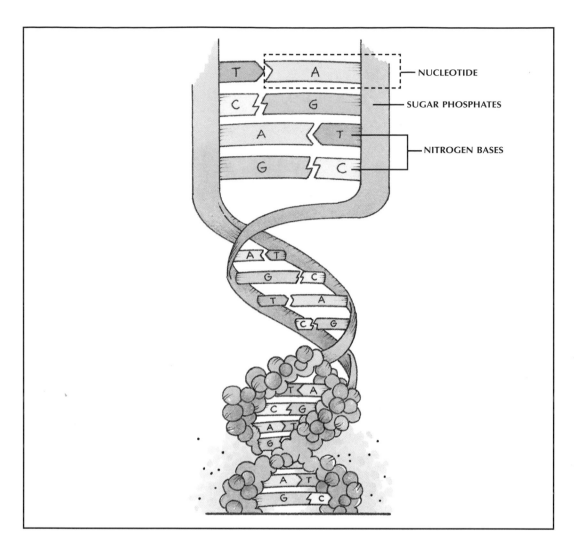

The structure of a DNA molecule

ral, or helix. It looks like a spiral staircase, with the nitrogen bases forming the steps and the sugar phosphates forming the sides. This double helix model of the DNA molecule was first worked out in 1953 by a British biochemist, Francis Crick, and his American colleague, James Watson.

Four kinds of nitrogen bases are found in DNA: adenine, thymine, guanine, and cytosine. (Usually abbreviated as A, T, G, and C, they are the four "letters" of the DNA alphabet.) They bond with each other according to very specific rules: A always pairs with T, and C pairs with G. So if you have a sequence on one strand such as ATCGTTA, then the corresponding part of the other strand

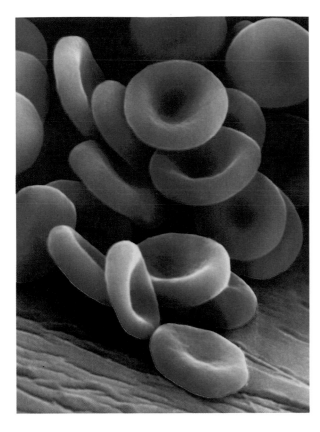

One combination of amino acids produces a red-colored protein called hemoglobin, which is found in red blood cells and carries oxygen to other cells throughout the body.

will be TAGCAAT. Normally, when scientists talk about a base sequence of DNA, they are referring to one strand, because once you know the order of the bases in the one, the pairing rules automatically tell you the sequence in the other strand.

Generally, each gene directs the production of a protein, and the proteins direct chemical reactions inside the cell or form body structures. DNA's instructions, expressed in the form of proteins, determine the traits of each organism. These instructions are spelled out in the four-letter alphabet of DNA's nitrogen bases, which is translated into **amino acids**, the building blocks of proteins.

There are twenty different kinds of amino acids. When the right kinds of amino acids are put together in the right amounts, they make a protein. Like Morse code and the English alphabet, the four DNA bases and the twenty different amino acids can each be used in various combinations to spell out a huge number of "words." For example, one combination of amino acids might spell out a protein called keratin, which forms your hair and fingernails.

How is the four-letter alphabet of DNA translated into the twenty-letter alphabet of the amino acids? A single gene is spelled out in combinations of three letters, each of which corresponds to one amino acid in a protein. The three-letter sequences are called **codons**. To translate DNA's message into proteins, the codons are first copied into another kind of nucleic acid, **RNA (ribonucleic acid)** .

✦ RNA'S ROLE ✦

As you know, the DNA's job is to store the master plans for everything that goes on in a living organism. But without RNA, these plans could never be carried out.

Like DNA, RNA is a long spiral chain made up of links containing a sugar, a phosphate, and a nitrogen base. The sugar is ribose, which is chemically very similar to the deoxyribose in DNA. Three of the four bases (A, C, and G) are the same as those found in DNA, but the fourth base is U (uracil), which is similar to but not exactly the same as the T (thymine) in DNA.

Unlike DNA, RNA has only a single strand of nucleotides. Its nitrogen bases are capable of forming chemical bonds, just like the DNA bases, but they normally do not link two RNA strands together. Instead, they form temporary bonds, either with parts of other RNA molecules or with parts of the DNA sequence, while they work to help DNA transmit its instructions to the cell. The bases in RNA follow the same pairing rules as those in DNA: A pairs with U (or with a T in DNA), and G pairs with C. When part of a DNA molecule is copied into RNA, the corresponding RNA bases are linked together. For example, if a portion of the base sequence on DNA is ACTTGA, the RNA copy will have UGAACU.

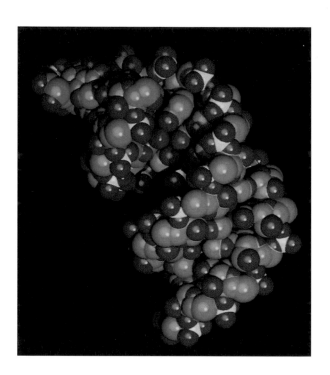

A computer-generated graphic of an RNA molecule shows that RNA is a long spiral linked together similar to DNA.

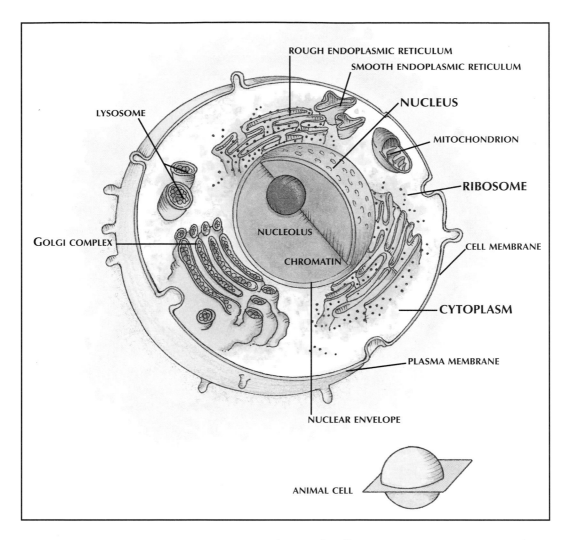

ROUGH ENDOPLASMIC RETICULUM

SMOOTH ENDOPLASMIC RETICULUM

NUCLEUS

MITOCHONDRION

RIBOSOME

CELL MEMBRANE

CYTOPLASM

PLASMA MEMBRANE

NUCLEAR ENVELOPE

LYSOSOME

GOLGI COMPLEX

NUCLEOLUS

CHROMATIN

ANIMAL CELL

A typical animal cell

Three kinds of RNA help DNA to translate its message into proteins: messenger RNA, ribosomal RNA, and transfer RNA. Here's how they work.

Parts of the DNA—genes—are continually turned on and off as the nucleus receives chemical messages from the rest of the cell and the world outside. The turned-on parts are copied into pieces of RNA that move out into the **cytoplasm**, the jellylike fluid outside the nucleus. This kind of RNA is called messenger RNA. The DNA message it carries is a set of instructions for making a protein. Messenger RNA waits at tiny ball-like structures, called **ribosomes**, the centers for manufacturing proteins, while amino acids are brought to it.

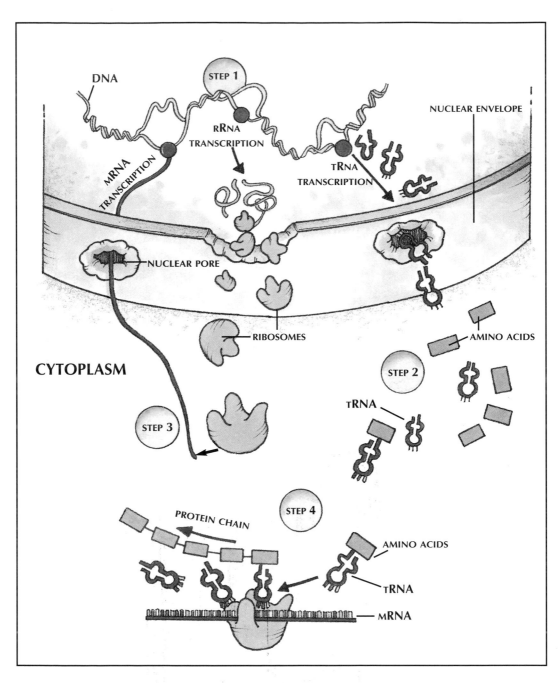

Inside the nucleus, portions of DNA are transcribed (step 1) into three main kinds of RNA: mRNA (messenger RNA), rRNA (ribosomal RNA), and tRNA (transfer RNA). These RNAs pass out into the cytoplasm, where different varieties of tRNA pick up amino acids (step 2) and carry them to ribosomes (containing rRNA) (step 3). There, amino acids are arranged according to the "message" spelled out in mRNA and joined to form a protein chain (step 4).

By the beginning of the 1960s, scientists had figured out that three-letter codons in DNA and RNA determine which amino acids will be built into proteins, but nobody knew exactly how the code worked. If you write down all the possible three-letter combinations in an alphabet of four letters (such as the A, U, C, and G in RNA), you will find that there are sixty-four of them. But there are only twenty different amino acids in most proteins. Are all the possible codons used? That would mean that more than one codon can correspond to the same amino acid.

In 1961, Marshall Nirenberg and Johann Matthaei made an artificial strand of RNA out of pure uracil and placed it in a solution of amino acids. The artificial RNA ("poly-U") promptly made a protein by stringing together molecules of just one amino acid, phenylalanine. So the codon UUU corresponds to phenylalanine. Other scientists quickly began making artificial RNA molecules and checking what amino acids each possible codon specified. By 1965, the entire genetic code had been worked out. Sixty-one of the sixty-four possible codons correspond to specific amino acids; the other three are "stop" signals that tell the ribosome to stop adding amino acids to the protein.

The genetic code allows for small errors in copying without any great harm to the protein. For example, if the codon GGU is miscopied, substituting an A for the U, it won't matter—the codon will still specify the same amino acid, glycine.

The cell has a special "taxicab service" to bring amino acids to the ribosomes to meet the messenger RNA with the plan for putting them together. The "taxicabs" are molecules of a different kind of RNA, called transfer RNA.

Transfer RNA molecules are much smaller than the messenger RNAs, and their job is much simpler. Messenger RNA carries the plans for a whole long protein molecule. But transfer RNA just has to pick up its own special amino acid and find its place on the messenger RNA molecule by lining up corresponding parts of the base sequence on the two kinds of RNA.

The ribosomes have their own RNA, called ribosomal RNA. This third type of RNA lines up the long messenger RNA molecules and helps to match them up with the right transfer RNA "taxicabs" carrying their amino acid passengers.

This is where those three-letter codons come in. As a protein starts to form, the end of a messenger RNA becomes attached to a ribosome. A transfer RNA molecule with a three-letter base sequence matching the first codon of the "message" lines up next to it, bringing its amino acid. Then the ribosome begins to move down the messenger RNA chain. Each time a space opens up, a transfer RNA with three nucleotides matching the next codon of the message moves in to fill it. Soon there is a whole row of transfer RNA molecules lined up next to messenger RNA. Each one is holding an amino acid. The amino acids link up together to form a chain of their own—a protein molecule. The sequence of amino acids in the new protein is determined by the sequence of bases in the messenger RNA. And it is the sequence of amino acids in the protein that determines what kind of protein it will be.

The growing protein molecule looks like a dangling tail as the ribosome moves on. Finally the ribosome gets to the end of the messenger RNA molecule and drops off. The new protein molecule breaks away and goes off to do its jobs in the cell.

✦ WHEN CELLS DIVIDE ✦

You started your life as a single cell. That cell divided and divided again and then became a ball of cells. As it got bigger, parts of it started to change. Soon there was a distinct head, body, and a little tail. Eventually, buds on the sides grew into arms and legs. Meanwhile, the body grew and the tail disappeared. Eyes, ears, nose, and mouth formed on the head. Inside the body, internal organs developed: a beating heart, lungs that weren't doing anything yet, stomach, and all the other structures that make up a human being.

For nine months you grew and developed inside your mother's body. Even after you were born, you continued to get bigger, and you will continue to grow and develop through your teen years. Through all this growth, from the first cell to a baby, a child, and finally an adult, the number of cells in the body increases. This happens by **cell division**, a process in which a single cell grows and splits into two cells. Even after growth has stopped, cell division is still important. When cells get injured or wear out, they need to be replaced. That's how you can heal when you cut your finger or break a leg. There are also certain cells that are constantly being produced. For instance, every time you touch something, you shed dead skin cells. Skin cells live for only about twenty-eight days. When they die, they have to be replaced by new skin cells. Red blood cells also have a short life span. They live for only a few months, and need to be replaced regularly.

Each new cell must have its own complete copy of DNA instructions. That means that all of the DNA must be copied before cell division takes place. First,

SECOND POSITION

		U	C	A	G	
	U	PHENYLALANINE	SERINE	TYROSINE	CYSTEINE	U
		PHENYLALANINE	SERINE	TYROSINE	CYSTEINE	C
		LEUCINE	SERINE	STOP	STOP	A
		LEUCINE	SERINE	STOP	TRYPTOPHAN	G
FIRST POSITION	**C**	LEUCINE	PROLINE	HISTIDINE	ARGININE	U
		LEUCINE	PROLINE	HISTIDINE	ARGININE	C
		LEUCINE	PROLINE	GLUTAMINE	ARGININE	A
		LEUCINE	PROLINE	GLUTAMINE	ARGININE	G
	A	ISOLEUCINE	THREONINE	ASPARAGINE	SERINE	U
		ISOLEUCINE	THREONINE	ASPARAGINE	SERINE	C
		ISOLEUCINE	THREONINE	LYSINE	ARGININE	A
		METHIONINE	THREONINE	LYSINE	ARGININE	G
	G	VALINE	ALANINE	ASPARTIC ACID	GLYCINE	U
		VALINE	ALANINE	ASPARTIC ACID	GLYCINE	C
		VALINE	ALANINE	GLUTAMIC ACID	GLYCINE	A
		VALINE	ALANINE	GLUTAMIC ACID	GLYCINE	G

THIRD POSITION

The twenty amino acids of proteins are not evenly represented in the genetic code. Three of them, leucine, arginine, and serine, are each specified by six different codons, while two amino acids, methionine and tryptophan, each have only one codon corresponding to them. The rest of the amino acids are coded by two, three, or four different codons. Another thing you might notice is that the codons for each particular amino acid generally have two letters in common. The codons for phenylalanine, for example, are UUU and UUC. If you think of codons as words, then UUU and UUC are synonyms, which both have the same meaning. The amino acid glycine has four synonyms in the code: GGU, GGC, GGA, and GGG.

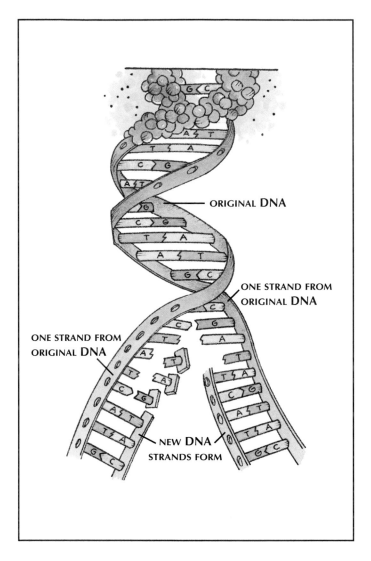

ORIGINAL **DNA**

ONE STRAND FROM ORIGINAL **DNA**

ONE STRAND FROM ORIGINAL **DNA**

NEW **DNA** STRANDS FORM

DNA replication

the coiled ladder of the DNA molecule starts to uncoil. The two sides then split down the middle at one end, like unzipping a zipper. The steps of the ladder, with their pairings of A with T, and C with G, are broken apart, leaving them without their partners. They are not alone for long. Floating freely around in the nucleus of the cell are As, Cs, Ts, and Gs. These bases are chemically drawn to their proper partners on the DNA strand. An **enzyme**, a special protein that helps make chemical reactions go, acts as a matchmaker, bringing the right bases together. As each base finds its respective partner—A with T, and C with G—they hook up, forming the steps on the DNA ladder. Now there are two completely identical DNA molecules where there was once one. Each new DNA molecule has one "old" strand and one newly assembled one. Each molecule can then twist itself back into a tightly coiled structure. The process by which DNA reproduces itself is referred to as **replication**.

Basically the same processes are used in making RNA copies of portions of DNA, but only part of the DNA is unzipped and only one strand is copied. When a portion of the DNA molecule is unzipped, RNA nucleotides pair up with the DNA bases and are assembled into a chain. Again, C pairs with G, but A pairs with U when RNA is being formed.

THREE

How Heredity Works

Has anyone ever told you, "You look just like your father," or "You have your mother's blue eyes"? If you look through your family album, you may notice that you also have your grandmother's curly hair or your uncle's nose. If you trace your family tree, you may find that you share similar characteristics with some of your relatives. It is true that we are all different—we look different, we sound different, we act differently. But all members in a family, from the ancient past to the present, may share some similarities; whether it's the shape of your nose or your bone structure, there could be parts of you that date back for generations. That's because all living things pass on their code of life—DNA—from generation to generation. You inherited DNA information from both your mother and your father. The DNA you received from your mother and father, in turn, contained information from their parents, and so on.

✦ CREATING A NEW LIFE ✦

Not all living things have a mother and a father. Take single-celled organisms, such as bacteria. When it comes to reproduction, a bacterium is more like a copy machine. First, a bacterium copies all of its DNA. Then it splits in half, forming two daughter cells. Usually the two daughter cells are identical twins: two cells that are exact copies of their parent, only smaller. With a complete set

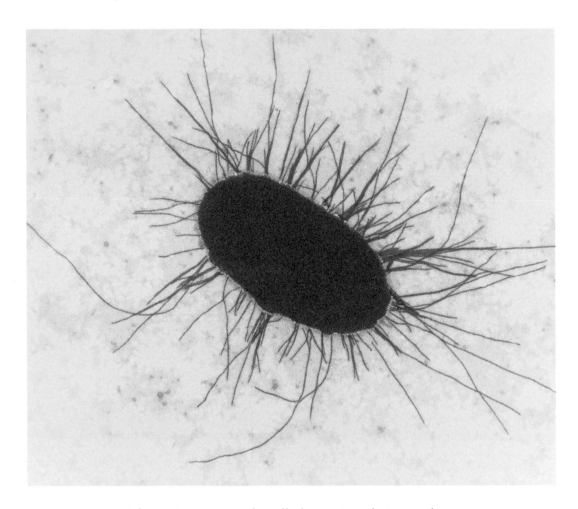

*A bacterium is a single-celled organism that reproduces
asexually by dividing in half to form two smaller replicas of itself.*

of genes and just the right building blocks, the two daughter cells can grow, and the cycle starts all over again.

More complex organisms, including humans, go from one generation to the next through a process called **sexual reproduction**. In this process, a male and a female from the same species combine some of their genetic material. Each of them produces special sex cells, which are used only for reproduction. The sex cells of a female are called eggs, or **ova**. Those of a male are called **sperm**. They are the key to sexual reproduction: A sex cell from a male joins with a sex cell from a female to form a single, combined cell that can develop into a whole new individual. This merging of two sex cells is called **fertilization**; the new cell (a fertilized egg) has a full set of DNA because it received a half set from each parent. So the new organism is not exactly like its mother or just like its father, but rather has a mixture of both of its parents' genes. As a result, a new, unique individual is born.

When the chromosome sets are divided during the formation of sex cells, it is pure luck which one of each chromosome pair will go to a particular egg or sperm. The result is that each parent's sex cell winds up with a *mixed* half-set of chromosomes: some that came from the father (the grandfather of the new offspring) and some from the mother (the new offspring's grandmother). When an egg and a sperm combine, they bring together a mixture of traits from all four grandparents. That is why children in the same family usually look rather similar but not exactly alike (unless they are identical twins, formed from the same fertilized egg).

Why do some people look similar to their mothers while some look more like their fathers or even their grandfathers? This is because we each pass on our DNA from one generation to the next. Hence, offspring are not exactly like either parent but, instead, share some of the traits of each.

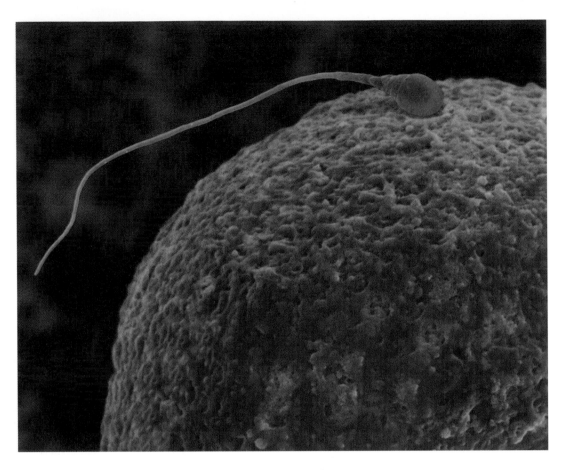

A male sex cell, or sperm, fertilizing a female sex cell, called an ovum, through the process of sexual reproduction.

In humans, all body cells (except the egg and sperm cells) have two sets of twenty-three chromosomes, making a total of forty-six. These chromosomes come in pairs—each chromosome in one set has a matching chromosome in the other set. The two chromosomes in a pair carry genes for the same traits, and these genes are arranged in the same order along the two DNA molecules.

Unlike normal body cells, egg cells and sperm cells have only one set of twenty-three chromosomes. So they have only one copy of each gene. When an egg and a sperm join to form the first cell of a new human being, the two sets of chromosomes (twenty-three from each parent) are combined. Now the new cell has forty-six chromosomes—one set of genes is from the mother, and one set is from the father.

What if people could reproduce the way bacteria or yeasts do, splitting off an offspring that is an exact genetic copy of its parent? This has been a favorite theme of science-fiction writers since the 1930s. But in 1996, science fiction became fact. Scottish researchers produced a lamb using the DNA from a body cell of an adult sheep. Dolly, the lamb, was a **clone**, essentially an identical twin of her "mother," the DNA donor.

The researchers had inserted the nucleus from her mother's cell into an egg cell from another sheep, after destroying the egg cell's own nucleus, then transplanted the egg cell into the uterus of an unrelated "surrogate mother" sheep. Inside the egg, genes in the nucleus that had been turned off for years were switched on, and the egg cell began to develop into an embryo, just as though it were a fertilized egg. Dolly, the clone, developed inside her foster mother's body according to the hereditary instructions of her genetic "mother," the sheep who provided the body-cell nucleus.

Researchers all over the world began to use the new cloning methods to produce clones of cows, pigs, and mice. Meanwhile, furious debates raged as people speculated on whether humans could, would, and should be cloned, too.

When people are expecting a baby, the big question is, "Will it be a boy or a girl?" Actually, that's up to the father. The half-set of chromosomes that he provides determines the sex of the baby. In fact, just one of his chromosomes makes the difference.

Most of the chromosomes are the same in both males and females. The difference lies in one special pair of chromosomes, called sex chromosomes. There are two sex chromosomes: the X chromosome and the Y chromosome.

In females, body cells contain two X chromosomes, which look exactly the same in size and shape. Males' sex chromosomes are not a matching pair. Their body cells have one X chromosome and a smaller Y chromosome. When the sex cells form, half of the sperm cells have an X chromosome and the other half have a Y chromosome. If a sperm carrying an X chromosome joins with an egg cell (which has its own X chromosome), then the offspring will be female (XX). But if a sperm carrying a Y chromosome joins with an egg cell, then the offspring will be a male (XY).

✦ UNEQUAL PARTNERS ✦

The laws of heredity were discovered by an Austrian monk named Gregor Mendel. He studied thousands of pea plants, which he grew in his monastery garden over a period of ten years starting in 1856. By crossing (mating) plants with different traits, such as green pods and yellow pods, Mendel deduced that traits are passed along from one generation to the next in tiny little "packages," which we now know as genes. Mendel found that two genes are responsible for each trait. The two genes in a pair may be different. Scientists call different forms of the same gene **alleles**.

The alleles that Mendel studied do not act like equal partners. Crossing tall pea plants with short ones, for example, produced only tall offspring, and a cross of green- and yellow-podded plants gave only green pods in the next generation. In each case one allele seemed to have a stronger influence in determining the traits of the offspring. Mendel called the stronger form **dominant**.

Today, Gregor Mendel is known as the "father of modern genetics," but during his lifetime very few people knew about him and his work. He published his results in the journal of the local natural history society, but they were ignored for over thirty years. Then, in 1900, an amazing coincidence occurred. Three scientists (Hugo de Vries in the Netherlands, Karl Correns in Germany, and Erich von Tschermak in Austria), each working independently, came up with a theory of heredity that was very similar to Mendel's. While checking the scientific literature on the subject, each researcher discovered Mendel's publications. All three published their own results as supporting evidence and gave Gregor Mendel full credit for the theory of genetics.

Gregor Mendel

PUNNETT SQUARES

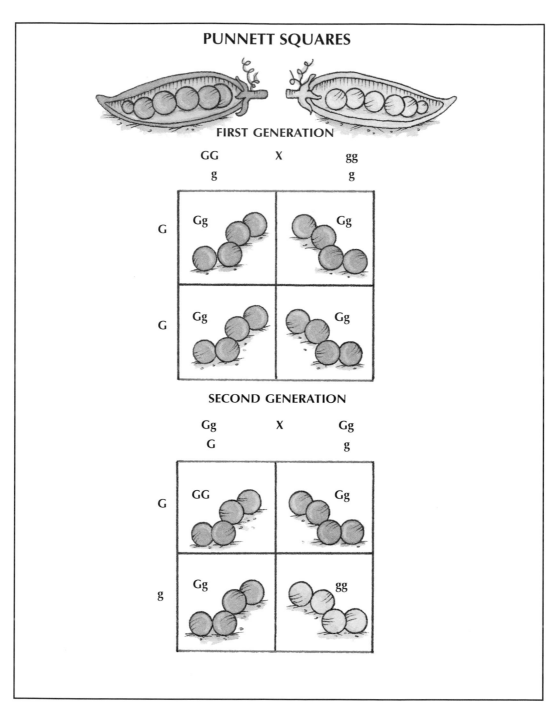

FIRST GENERATION

GG   X   gg

g   g

	G	g
G	Gg	Gg
G	Gg	Gg

SECOND GENERATION

Gg   X   Gg

G   g

	G	g
G	GG	Gg
g	Gg	gg

The expected results of a cross of two different genotypes can be determined by using a simple diagram called a Punnett square. The mother's genotype is at the left, and the father's genotype at the top. The possible combinations in the first and second generations are shown in the four boxes of the squares.

The dominant trait is the one that appeared in the **hybrid** (mixed) offspring. Mendel used the term **recessive** for the trait that did not show up in the hybrid offspring. The recessive trait reappeared in the next generation when the hybrid plants were crossed. Later scientists coined the terms **phenotype** for the appearance of a trait and **genotype** for the combination of alleles that is responsible for the trait. A dominant trait will show up in the phenotype whether the genotype has one or two of those alleles. A recessive trait will appear, however, only if the recessive allele is inherited from both parents.

The laws that Mendel discovered in experiments on peas hold true for other plants and animals, as well—including humans. For example, if a woman with black hair (who comes from an all-black-haired family) marries a man with blond hair, all their children are likely to have black hair. The phenotype of black hair color is produced by a dark-colored pigment, melanin, and the production of this pigment is a dominant trait. But two black-haired people can have a blond child if they both have a mixed genotype.

For many traits the patterns of inheritance are not quite so simple. In some plant species, unlike Mendel's peas, the color of the flowers in hybrid offspring is not like that of the dominant parent but a blending of the colors of the two parents. Purebred plants with red flowers, for example, when crossed with purebred plants with white flowers, give hybrid offspring with pink flowers. In such cases the dominance of one allele over the other is not complete.

Confusing patterns of heredity also result when a trait is determined by more than one pair of alleles. A brown-eyed mother and a blue-eyed father, for example, are likely to have children with brown eyes. (Like hair color, dark eye color is produced by melanin.) But the children may have blue eyes (if the mother has a hybrid genotype) or gray, green, or hazel eyes, because other genes also are involved. At least ten different genes determine human skin color, so children in the same family can have skin of quite different shades. There is even another set of alleles that can influence hair color: A gene for an orange pigment can produce various shades of red hair, depending on how much melanin the hair contains.

The seven traits that Mendel studied in pea plants are all inherited independently. A tall plant, for example, can have either green or yellow pods and either smooth or wrinkled seeds. So can a short plant. Scientists later discovered that each of the seven traits is on a different one of the pea plant's seven pairs of chromosomes. But what happens if the genes for two traits are on the same chromosome? In the early 1900s, researchers discovered that certain traits always seemed to be inherited together. For example, fruit flies with the usual red eyes have normal-size wings, but fruit flies with white eyes have wings that are much smaller than normal. Soon it was realized that the genes for these **linked traits** are found on the same chromosome.

Careful studies on large numbers of animals and plants revealed that linked traits are not quite *always* inherited together. In any large number of crosses studying the eye color and wing size of fruit flies, for example, there will be a few offspring that have white eyes and normal-size wings and a few with red eyes and tiny wings. The reason is that when the chromosomes pair up while a cell is dividing, they temporarily join at the middle and their dangling ends may cross over each other. Sometimes the chromosomes break at the crossover point. The cell's repair enzymes quickly put them back together, but sometimes they accidentally attach the broken pieces to the wrong chromosomes.

Each chromosome in the pair now has some genes from the mother and some from the father. **Crossing over** is thus another way of adding genetic variety to the new offspring. It also gives scientists a tool for determining the relative positions of genes on a chromosome. The closer two genes are, the more likely they are to be inherited together. If there is a large distance between two genes on the same chromosome, chances are greater that crossing over may occur, and they are more likely to be inherited separately. Scientists have used the results of crosses involving linked traits to draw chromosome maps showing the sequence of genes along each chromosome.

Still more genetic variety is added by **jumping genes**, segments of DNA that can move from one position on the chromosome to another, or even to a different chromosome. In some cases the gene works fine in its new location. Sometimes, however, in its new site the gene is controlled by switches or modifiers that change its effects or stop it from working. They might result in genetic disorders.

Recently researchers have discovered that small molecules of RNA help to control when and how genes are expressed. In the early 1990s, researchers at Dartmouth Medical School were working with mutants of a small worm called *C. elegans*, whose development stopped at an early stage. The gene responsible for this problem was isolated in 1993, and to the researchers' surprise it coded for an RNA molecule that turned off some of the genes involved in the worm's development. Later similar genes were discovered in other organisms, from flies to fish and even humans. Geneticists now believe that there may be hundreds or even thousands of different kinds of small RNA molecules in each genome, helping to control other genes and doing various jobs in the cell. Some of them seem to be formed on patterns provided by the introns—the bits of DNA that are snipped out when coding genes are edited by the cell. Others may come from parts of the "junk DNA," whose functions are just beginning to be discovered. Researchers in a number of laboratories are entering this exciting new field, hunting for new RNA genes and exploring the functions of the RNA molecules they make.

♦ FOUR ♦

WHEN THE CODE GOES WRONG

The DNA in each cell in your body contains an incredible amount of information. If all this information could be recorded on paper, there would be enough to fill a thousand books of five hundred pages each. New cells are being formed in your body all the time. Each of these cells contains the same set of plans, or DNA. Every time a single cell divides to form two new ones, its DNA is copied; so there are two identical sets, one for each daughter cell.

The copying of DNA in the cell is amazingly accurate. If you copied ten pages from a book and made only one mistake, you would be doing very well. But a cell makes only about one mistake in every *million* pages when it duplicates its DNA. Just where the copy error occurs on the chromosome makes a big difference. If it happens inside one of the stretches of junk DNA, it may have no effect at all. But if the change occurs in a gene with important instructions, it can cause a big problem.

When a parent cell makes one of these rare errors in copying its DNA, a daughter cell will have a set of DNA that is slightly different from those of the other cells. Such a change in the DNA is called a **mutation**. The daughter cell will pass on the mutation to its own daughters when it divides, and they may pass it on in turn.

Mutations are changes in the plans that the DNA carries. If a mutation occurs in one of the early cells that starts off the life of a new baby, the plans of development may be terribly upset. This may cause problems in the production of important proteins. The baby may be born with some kind of anomaly, such as missing fingers or toes, or serious diseases can result.

✦ KINDS OF MUTATIONS ✦

Mutations are changes in the sequence of bases in genes. Mutations can occur in a number of different ways. For instance, the **substitution** of a single base—replacing the correct base with an incorrect one—may not have much effect, but if this kind of mutation results in a change in the amino acid in a key part of a

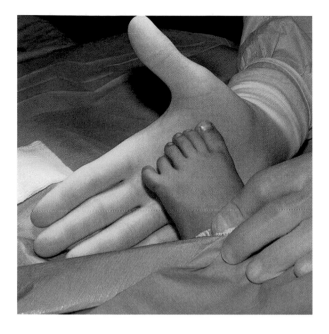

A mutation in the DNA of this child resulted in polydactyly, a condition of having more than the normal number of fingers or toes. The condition is usually corrected with surgery.

protein, it can change the nature of the protein. A number of diseases have been found to result from a change in just one base in a gene.

Some mutations may result in the **deletion** (removal) of one or more bases. Bases may also be inserted or added to the DNA chain. Unless there is a deletion or **insertion** of exactly three bases or a multiple of three, the codons after the change are not going to read properly. For example, take the code ATT TAG CAT GAG. If the A in the second codon is deleted, the "reading frame" of the codon sequence gets shifted. Now the message will read: ATT TGC ATG AG. All the "words" (codons) after the deletion got garbled, and the message no longer makes sense.

Another type of mutation is known as **translocation**. Translocations occur when a piece of a chromosome breaks off and then reattaches—not to where it belongs, but to some other chromosome. Depending on where it broke, the effects differ. The genes may work perfectly well in their new location. Or they may be influenced by other genes on the new chromosome, and the way they work may be changed. If a break occurs in the middle of the gene, the whole gene may stop working completely.

Mutations may also involve changes in the number of chromosomes. For instance, things may go wrong in the process of cell division that produces the sex cells. The chromosome sets may not separate properly, causing one sex cell to get an extra chromosome, while another is missing one. If that sex cell joins with one of the opposite sex to start a new life, the cells of the new organism may have three of a particular chromosome or only one instead of the normal pair.

✦ GENETIC DISORDERS ✦

Researchers have identified more than 4,000 hereditary diseases and disorders—conditions that are due to changes in the genes and can be passed on from one generation to another. Medical experts have put these disorders into three main categories: single-gene disorders, multifactorial disorders, and chromosome disorders.

Single-gene disorders include conditions that involve just one gene mutation. For example, sickle-cell anemia is a condition that develops when a single letter in the gene for hemoglobin is copied incorrectly. This small change causes a problem in the shape of the red blood cells, which are needed to carry oxygen throughout the body. These odd-shaped cells can be damaged easily, and can greatly reduce the number of red blood cells. They may also pile up in clumps, clogging blood vessels and damaging them.

A person can carry the sickle-cell gene without actually developing the illness. In fact, this **carrier** of the gene may not even know he or she has it. However, a child can develop the disease if he or she receives two copies of the mutated gene: one copy from the mother and one from the father. This disease is a recessive trait. It will show up only when two copies of the mutation come together.

Huntington's disease is another genetic illness that involves a single gene mutation. Unlike sickle-cell anemia, however, this mutation is dominant. So a child can develop this disease even if only one parent is carrying the Huntington's gene. Huntington's disease is a fatal illness that gradually destroys the parts of the brain that control body movements. People who are carrying the Huntington's gene may not even realize they have it until years after they have given birth to children of their own. Strangely, the defect in the gene (a repetition of the bases CAG) seems to multiply when it is passed down from one generation to the next, causing symptoms to be more severe and appear at an earlier age, generation after generation.

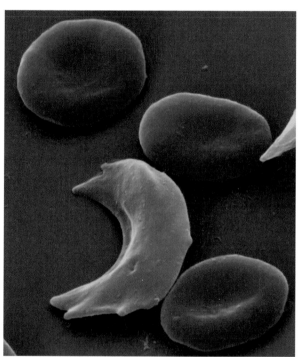

Normally, red blood cells look like round doughnuts without the hole in the middle, but when a person has sickle-cell anemia, the red blood cells take on a crescent, or sickle, shape.

Single-gene disorders also include sex-linked disorders, caused by a mutation on the X chromosome. One example is hemophilia, in which the blood does not clot properly and a person can bleed to death from a minor cut. Hemophilia occurs most often in males. Females can carry the hemophilia gene,

Most single-gene disorders are quite rare, affecting fewer than 1 in 2,000 people. But they may be much more common in certain groups of the population. Sickle-cell anemia, for example, affects 1 out of every 500 African Americans. Among Caucasians, the most common genetic disease is cystic fibrosis, in which thick mucus accumulates in the lungs and makes breathing difficult. In about 70 percent of cases, this disease is due to a deletion of three bases in a gene; the other 30 percent are due to more than 300 different defects in the same gene. Cystic fibrosis occurs in 1 out of 2,000 Caucasians in the United States, and about 1 in 22 is a carrier of a mutant cystic fibrosis gene.

but most do not develop the disease. Because this a recessive trait, a female gets it only if she has inherited *two* hemophilia genes, one from each parent. Female carriers can, however, pass this mutant gene down to future generations. As a result, sons and grandsons may develop hemophilia.

Multifactorial disorders include genetic conditions that develop as a result of multiple genes, or a combination of genetic and environmental influences. Some common examples are physical challenges such as clubfoot and cleft palate. These disorders tend to occur in families, but they do not show clear patterns of heredity. In fact, it is sometimes difficult to determine whether they are really genetic or purely environmental.

Chromosomal disorders develop when there is a problem with an entire chromosome, instead of just one or a few genes. Down syndrome, in which a person receives an extra chromosome, is the most common example of this kind

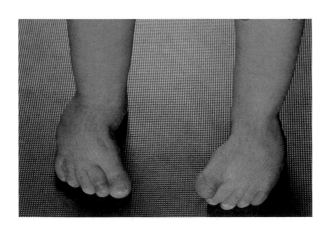

The most common type of clubfoot is shown here. The heel is turned inward, and the rest of the foot is bent downward and inward. This can be corrected with splints or surgery.

of mutation. Normally, people get two copies of chromosome 21 (one from the mother and one from the father). People with Down syndrome receive three copies (two from one parent, one from the other) because the chromosomes were not divided up properly during the cell division that formed the sex cells. So instead of having the usual total of forty-six chromosomes in each body cell, a person with Down syndrome has forty-seven chromosomes. Down syndrome is apparent at birth, and people with this disorder have a characteristic physical appearance. Developmental disabilities are also a common sign, although they may range from mild to severe. Other physical challenges may develop as well.

GENETIC BUT NOT HEREDITARY

When a mutation occurs in a body cell, it may result in disease. Too much exposure to sunlight, for example, may cause changes in the DNA of skin cells that damage the normal controls over their growth and division. The cells begin to multiply uncontrollably—they have turned into cancer cells. Scientists have discovered a number of genes that are associated with cancer. Some of these genes, called **oncogenes**, actually cause cells to turn "outlaw," but others protect against cancer. (Cancer results when the protective genes are damaged or lost.) Some types of cancer are hereditary, but skin cancers caused by sun damage to DNA in skin cells are not.

✦ GENETIC TESTING ✦

If there were a test that could determine whether you are carrying the genes for a deadly disease that could strike you ten years from now, would you want to take the test? What about a test that could predict your chances of having a child with some disabling or fatal disorder?

Genetics has come a long way since Mendel's time. We now have genetic testing that can determine a person's risk of developing genetic disorders later in life. There are also ways to estimate the likelihood that a couple will have a child with a genetic disorder, and even ways to check on a baby's potential health months before it is born, determining whether it has any of several hundred different inherited disorders.

Since genes determine the production of proteins, genetic diseases usually involve a change that results in a protein that does not work properly, or is not produced at all. In some cases, tests for the protein in blood or skin cells can reveal not only people who have the disorder, but also people who are carrying the recessive gene for it. Tay-Sachs disease, for example, is a serious illness that results in death at an early age. Babies born with it lack an enzyme called hex A. Without this key enzyme, a chemical builds up in nerve cells and eventually destroys them. Blood tests can show if prospective parents have the gene because carriers produce smaller than usual amounts of hex A.

Chromosome disorders, such as Down syndrome, can be detected by examining the chromosome set of cells from a developing **fetus,** obtained by drawing out a sample of fluid through a needle inserted into the mother's abdomen. Similar tests on prospective parents can determine whether the parents are carrying chromosomes with particular defects that have been linked with genetic diseases.

DNA testing has made it possible to detect far more genetic disorders, both in prospective parents and in their children. In a blood or tissue sample, researchers use special **restriction enzymes** that act like chemical scissors to cut up the DNA. This produces fragments of varying lengths, which are sorted by a technique called **electrophoresis**. The DNA fragments move at different speeds along a layer of gel under the influence of electric current. A banded pattern similar to a bar code is produced in the gel, determined by the particular assortment of DNA fragments. Scientists call these fragments **RFLPs** (pronounced "rifflips"). The RFLP patterns are different for each person (individual "fingerprints"), but parts of the patterns are similar among members of the same family. Some of them are typically found in people with particular genetic disorders and thus can be used to screen for these disorders.

Restriction enzymes can also be used to snip out particular defective genes in a sample taken from someone with a genetic disorder. These genes can then be mixed with a blood or tissue sample. If the person has a copy of the gene for that disorder, the test gene lines up with that part of the chromosome and bonds to it.

✦ WHAT GOOD IS GENETIC TESTING? ✦

The purpose of genetic testing is to determine whether a person carries a mutation that can lead to a serious genetic condition. It does not, however, show that the person will develop the disease. He or she could be a carrier, and pass the trait down to future generations. Environmental influences may also play a role in transmission.

If genetic testing can't tell you whether or not you will develop a disease, then why bother? First of all, if you know that you are at risk, you may be able to spot symptoms right away. For many diseases, early treatment can be a life-saver. A condition called PKU, for example, can be detected by a simple chemical test on a spot of urine in a newborn baby's diaper. Someone with PKU does not have the enzyme to handle one of the amino acids commonly found in foods. A toxic product called phenyl ketone builds up in the brain, and the child becomes developmentally challenged. But if such a child is identified early and fed a special diet, he or she will develop normally.

Genetic testing is also a good tool for people who worry about transmitting mutant genes to their offspring. When a woman who carries mutant genes finds a prospective mate who is a match for one of these "bad" genes, any potential children could inherit a pair of dangerous recessive genes and develop a genetic disorder. People who are at risk for a disorder may seek genetic counseling. A genetic counselor will analyze the clients' family history and DNA test results. He or she will also help the clients understand what the genetic test results mean, and interpret the risks for developing the disease. For example, if a man and a woman both have a mutant gene for cystic fibrosis, they have a 25 percent chance of giving birth to a child who will receive both copies of the cystic fibrosis gene and, therefore, develop the disease. This doesn't mean that if this couple has four children, then just one of them will have cystic fibrosis. It means that *each* child has a one in four chance of developing the disease.

Some parents do not want to take a chance in passing on mutant genes to their children. There are other options, which may include adoption or in vitro fertilization: An egg is fertilized with sperm in a laboratory dish and inserted into a woman's uterus for developing. If the husband's sperm is used, the embryo is tested for the disease gene before implanting. The mother's egg may also be tested and used.

✦ FIVE ✦

THE GENOME PROJECT

Everything that makes you who you are, from eye color to a tendency for baldness or allergies, is all stored in your body's book of life—your DNA. Scientists refer to the total DNA in an organism as its **genome**. (The term "genome" comes from blending the two words *gene* and *chromosome*.) Researchers believe that if they can figure out the human genome, then they may be able to get to the root of genetic disorders—errors in the genes or chromosomes. Then they can design techniques to fix the errors in the code before they turn into a problem.

✦ FOCUSING ON THE HUMAN GENOME ✦

Can you imagine trying to read the instruction manual that makes up the human genome? It contains more than 3 billion chemical base pairs! But that's exactly what researchers had in mind when the Human Genome Project was created in October 1990. With funding provided by the U.S. government, the Human Genome Project had one main focus: to *map* and *sequence* all of the DNA in human chromosomes. To make a genetic map, researchers needed to figure out which genes belong to which chromosomes and where each gene lies on that chromosome. Then they had to figure out the DNA sequence—the specific order of As, Cs, Ts, and Gs in the entire genome: TAATCG . . . , etc. They aimed to reach their goal by 2005.

While researchers at the Human Genome Project, headed by Francis Collins, were diligently working toward their goal, another team of researchers, led by J. Craig Venter, was also trying to figure out the human genome, using private funding. Venter had worked on decoding genes for the National Institutes of Health (NIH), but found the methods used at NIH very slow. Frustrated, Venter joined a private research firm that provided him with state-of-the-art equipment to speed up the process in identifying the chemical letters in DNA. There, he and his colleagues were able to decode the genome of the first free-living organism—a bacterium. By 1998, Venter headed up a new company, called Celera Genomics, where he had access to powerful gene-sequencing machines. He now had his sights on the human genome, and he declared that the sequencing would be complete by 2001, four years earlier than the goal of the Human Genome Project. So the race was on. Which team would be the first to crack the human genetic code? In June 2000, Venter and Collins independently reached their goals around the same time.

Now that researchers have figured out the "spelling" of the chromosomes, the next step is to identify the genes and what they do. This will be no easy task. Much of the human genome—as much as 97 percent—is made up of junk DNA. Sprinkled among it are the genes, which contain the useful information. Researchers will have to weed out the junk to locate the key genes.

Why is it so important to decode the human genome? Scientists hope that by learning exactly where the genes are and what they do, they will be able to control the actions of key genes. For example, they may be able to "turn off" genes that contribute to obesity or strengthen the signals of those that prevent cancer growth. Pharmaceutical companies hope to come up with effective new medicines to fight diseases. "[If] you understand how the gene works," says Francis Collins, "you understand how its misspelling results in the risk of disease, and then you can develop a molecule, a small molecule, a drug molecule that tweaks the system just right to compensate for that."

With the ability to map a person's genome, doctors of the not-too-distant future will also be able to tailor treatment plans to each individual patient, choosing drugs that will be most effective and cause the fewest side effects for someone with a particular combination of genes.

✦ GENOMES OF OTHER SPECIES ✦

Since the human genome project began, researchers have studied the genomes of other species as well. They have worked out the genomes for as many as

On June 26, 2000, Venter and Collins made a joint announcement at a ceremony in the White House explaining they had each completed a first draft of the human genome sequence. Venter (left) and Collins are seen here with President Bill Clinton.

forty different kinds of organisms, including bacteria, fruit flies, yeasts, worms, plants, and mice.

Scientists have completed the first genome sequence of a plant, *Arabidopsis thaliana*, a tiny weed related to the mustard plant. It is not a useful crop, but it's easy to study in the laboratory because its genome is small (125 million base pairs compared to our 3 billion), and it multiplies very quickly, producing up to

Before the human genome map was completed, it was generally accepted that humans had a total of 100,000 genes. The first draft of the human genome investigation suggested that the number is much lower—around 30,000 to 35,000 genes. (Later data indicated that this estimate might be too low, and the actual total may be between 50,000 and 70,000.) By comparison, a roundworm has about 19,000 genes, and the fruit fly *Drosophila* has 13,000 genes. Single-celled bacteria have far fewer genes. *Haemophilus influenzae*, the bacterium sequenced by Craig Venter, has only 1,743 genes, and mycoplasmas, the smallest living things, have fewer than 500 genes.

Arabidopsis *could even be used to help human diseases. Nearly 150 genes in this plant are similar to genes associated with diseases in humans.*

one million plants in a year. Scientists believe that this plant can be a model for all other plants. Researchers have found 100 genes in *Arabidopsis* that could be used to create new herbicides. Other genes may help plants to become resistant to frost and drought.

Researchers hope that the study of mice will be important in working out the human genome. Amazingly, about 80 percent of the mouse genome is almost exactly the same as the corresponding genes in humans. Researchers are tinkering with mouse genes, perhaps eliminating ("knocking out") one or changing a base or two, and then studying what effects these changes produce. For example, "knockout mice" lacking one of the genes needed to

Researchers have also been working on the rice genome, which has about 430 million base pairs. Rice is an important crop for half the world's population, but it lacks some important nutrients. Once the rice genome is mapped, scientists may be able to introduce genes to produce new varieties of rice that are supplemented with nutrients, such as vitamin A, to prevent blindness. This preventable disease currently strikes 5,000 to 6,000 children each year, especially in places like Asia, where vitamin A-rich foods are not a normal part of the diet.

form the eye develop cataracts (a clouding of the eye lens that results in blindness). Once the function of a mouse gene has been determined, it can be compared to the sequence in the human genome, and this may provide insights into human disorders.

Why do some people get sick when exposed to disease germs, while others can fight them off? Researchers have found genes in mice associated with the ability to fight off disease germs. Other mouse genes have been found to be involved in gaining excessive weight (obesity). A tendency toward alcoholism has also been linked to certain genes in mice. The knowledge gained in studying mice can provide a better understanding of these conditions in humans.

✦ SIX ✦

THE DNA DETECTIVE

Have you ever looked at your own fingerprints? If you press your fingertips against an ink pad and then press them firmly on a piece of paper, you will see patterns of curvy lines, loops, and whorls. Have a friend make his or her own fingerprints. Then compare your fingerprints to your friend's. Can you spot any differences in the patterns?

Fingerprints are like your very own personal ID card. No two people have the same fingerprints. In fact, police have used fingerprinting for identification purposes since the 1890s. Over the years, many criminals have been caught when police officers dusted for "prints" at the crime scene and matched them with those of a suspect. But what if a criminal wears gloves and doesn't leave any fingerprints? Fingerprints can also be altered through surgery.

These days, criminal investigations are depending more and more on a different kind of "fingerprint" that cannot be changed—DNA fingerprinting. No two people have the same DNA, except for identical twins.

> ### DID YOU KNOW?
>
> About 99.8 percent of your DNA is exactly the same as everyone else's. But in a genome of 3 billion letters, even that two-tenths of a percent translates into 6 million separate spelling differences. The variations in the letter sequences are what makes us so different from one another.

Earlier we discussed the techniques used to turn a DNA sample into a personal bar code, similar to those you see in supermarkets. These personal DNA "fingerprints" were originally used to detect genetic disorders by finding characteristic patterns linked to particular traits. It was not until the mid-1980s that DNA fingerprinting started to be used in criminal investigations. A sample of DNA can be extracted from hair, blood, saliva, sweat, or other bodily materials. (When you turn a doorknob, for example, you leave behind thousands of dead skin cells, which could be used for DNA testing.) If the DNA fingerprint from this

---

COPY MACHINE

Sometimes there's not a lot of evidence left at a crime scene. There may be just a drop of blood or a single strand of hair. In cases like these, the sample may not be big enough for electrophoresis testing. So researchers use a technique called **PCR**, which works somewhat like a copy machine. PCR stands for polymerase chain reaction. A DNA polymerase, an enzyme involved in making new copies of DNA, is used to copy a small segment of DNA over and over again (a chain reaction). Millions of exact copies are produced, giving the testers more materials to work with.

---

sample is identical to the one taken from a suspect, then there is a high probability that they came from the same person.

DNA fingerprinting has been used to solve various crimes. For instance, the DNA in the dried saliva from a stamp led to the arrest of the Unabomber, who anonymously mailed packages containing bombs that exploded when the packages were opened by unsuspecting victims. DNA testing has also freed people who have been wrongfully convicted of murder or rape.

DNA fingerprinting can be used to determine whether two people are related to each other. For instance, DNA matches have allowed immigrants to stay in the United States legally when genetic tests showed that they were related to a resident. These tests have also been used in paternity suits, when there is a question of who is really the father of a child.

DNA tests have revealed the identities of unknown Vietnam War veterans two decades after they died. In 1994, the military started a campaign to collect DNA samples from every member of the armed forces. The samples were stored in freezers and recorded in computer bases. Officials hoped that this would cut down the number of unidentified soldiers in the future.

The chances of DNA results being inaccurate are one in 70 billion. People are identified by the sequence of base pairs in their DNA. But there are billions of base pairs in the genome, far too many for scientists to test, so how can the results be so accurate? Researchers use only a small number of short segments of the total DNA sequence, but they target those that are known to vary greatly among individuals. When the patterns of these sequences in one sample are identical to those in another sample, there is a match.

✦ DNA REVEALS CLUES TO THE PAST ✦

DNA testing has become a useful tool for gaining knowledge about organisms that have existed both in the past and in the present. Scientists use DNA testing to classify organisms; to determine evolutionary relationships among animals, plants, and even humans; and to choose suitable mates for captive endangered species.

Researchers have been able to take DNA samples from ancient specimens and compare them to samples from present-day creatures. It is especially helpful when these organisms have been preserved. For instance, ancient insects have

---

THE OTHER DNA

The DNA in the chromosomes spells out an organism's genome, but this is not the only DNA an organism has. Each cell contains hundreds of structures called **mitochondria**, in which energy is generated for the cell's needs by breaking the chemical bonds in sugar molecules. The mitochondria have their own "instruction manual," a set of DNA that is inherited separately from the chromosomes in the cell nucleus. Researchers use both kinds of DNA in tracing relationships. Mitochondrial DNA (mtDNA), however, gives information only about the mother's heredity. Mitochondria are passed on from one generation to the next in the egg cells of the female parent; sperm contain only chromosomal DNA.

A mosquito preserved in amber

been preserved in amber, the hardened resin of certain types of trees. Researchers at the American Museum of Natural History used DNA testing to study a very large termite found encased in amber dated to about 3 million years ago. This ancient specimen was found to be closely related to modern termites. In one gene, for example, only nine out of one hundred base pairs differed between the ancient and modern species. Comparisons of DNA also allowed the researchers to trace the ancient termite's evolutionary relationships to modern termites, as well as to other insects, including roaches and preying mantises.

It is rare for animals' flesh and soft tissues to be preserved. However, frozen remains of woolly mammoths have been found in Siberia and Alaska. In the early 1980s, scientists examined genetic material taken from a mammoth and found that the DNA in these creatures was more similar to that of Asian elephants than to that of African elephants.

Recently, researchers removed DNA from the upper-arm bone of a Neanderthal fossil to compare it with that of modern humans. They found that the Neanderthals were not our ancestors. There were significant differences—about twenty-seven mutations. These findings suggest that humans and Neanderthals split from a common ancestor about 500,000 to 600,000 years ago. As for our more recent history, comparisons of the DNA of living people from present-day Europe and Africa suggest that Europe was settled about 25,000 years ago by a few hundred people from Africa. Similarities in genetic patterns show that these people all came from the same group of ancestors, while the differences indicate how long ago the immigrants to Europe separated from the rest of the African population. "It is remarkable how the human chromosomes can be read as a history book," commented MIT geneticist Eric Lander, the leader of the study.

SEVEN

TINKERING WITH DNA

Scientists have learned a great deal about how DNA and genes work. Now they are using their knowledge to try to manipulate the chemicals of heredity. One goal is to correct the defects that produce genetic disorders. Another is to improve on agricultural plants and animals to produce bigger yields or more nutritious foods. Tinkering with genes can also provide new sources of disease-fighting drugs and other valuable materials, using specially modified bacteria, plants, or animals as "factories." In fact, the original aim of the Scottish researchers who first cloned a sheep was to develop ways of mass-producing genetically modified animals without the uncertainties of breeding.

✦ GENETIC ENGINEERING ✦

The genetic knowledge gained since the 1950s has made it possible for scientists to "engineer" living organisms, changing their genes to produce special characteristics in their offspring. For instance, they have inserted genes into plants to increase their resistance to diseases, or to make them able to grow in harsh environments. Scientists have also produced genetically engineered plants that are resistant to insect damage. This can help to cut down on the use of pesticides, which can be harmful to humans and the environment. For example, organic farmers (farmers who don't use pesticides) have been using a kind of bacteria, called Bt, for pest control. These microscopic organisms are harmless to people and to the environment, but poisonous to insects. An insect doesn't die right after taking a bite out of a plant that has been sprayed with Bt. As it starts to digest the Bt-contaminated food, the bacteria release a poison that eventually kills the pest.

Instead of spraying Bt on plants, genetic engineers have taken the "poison" gene from the bacterium and inserted it into food crops. For instance, the Monsanto company has created genetically altered potatoes that contain the Bt gene, in an effort to save them from Colorado potato beetles, which are major pests to the potato plant. Monsanto has also genetically engineered corn plants to be resistant to the corn borer, an insect pest that often damages the inside of the stalk, which cannot be reached by pesticides. Each cell of these genetically engineered plants contains the Bt gene so that the plants are fully protected against insect pests.

Back in 1994, the first genetically engineered plant was sold in supermarkets. It was called the FLAVR SAVR Tomato. The idea was to create a tomato that would handle the long, bumpy ride from the farm to the stores without getting soft and bruised. Usually, tomatoes have to be picked while still green to keep them in good condition. But some people complain that tomatoes picked when they are unripe are not fresh and do not taste good.

A GENETIC SHORTCUT

For thousands of years, people have been aware that living things pass down their traits from one generation to the next, even though they didn't know about genes and how they work. Dog breeders, for example, carefully selected animals with specific traits to produce offspring with the traits of their parents. That's how the many dog breeds, such as dachshunds, Great Danes, and Chihuahuas, have evolved. Even today, farmers select and crossbreed many different kinds of fruits and vegetables we eat every day.

It can take some time for desired traits to appear, however. To speed up the process, genetic engineers have figured out which genes determine particular traits. Then in a laboratory, they chemically insert the desired gene into an animal or plant. So genetic engineering is not really new and revolutionary but rather a kind of shortcut for what animal and plant breeders have been doing all along—selecting for favorable genes.

To create this product, scientists removed the gene that makes tomatoes become overripe. Then they inserted a gene with the opposite "spelling"—A instead of T, C in place of G, and so on. This **antisense** gene knocks out the action of the original gene, so the tomato does not become overripe and, therefore, has a longer shelf life. When the FLAVR SAVR Tomato was introduced to the public, there were mixed reactions. Some people called it "Frankenfood," while others thought that it was just a new and improved tomato. However, this genetically altered tomato was sold for only a year, because it was found that it wasn't tough enough to handle the rough trip to the market after all.

Since 1986, over 2,000 genetically engineered plants have been developed around the world, and efforts will most likely continue in years to come. Critics

Controversy surrounded the use of Bt in 1999, when researchers found that monarch caterpillars died after eating the pollen from genetically engineered corn. Some scientists feared that widespread planting of Bt corn could greatly harm the monarch population. Later studies cast doubt on the original findings.

An estimated 60 to 70 percent of the foods sold in supermarkets in the United States contain ingredients made from genetically engineered crops.

say that genetic engineering is unsafe and unproven. The Food and Drug Administration (FDA) says that genetically altered foods are no different from the originals chemically, nutritionally, and in terms of safety.

✦ HOW GENE TINKERING WORKS ✦

How do scientists change a gene? They use a technique called **gene-splicing**. Restriction enzymes are used to separate the DNA molecule. These chemical scissors cut up the DNA at certain points. A piece of the DNA is isolated from an organism and *spliced* (joined) to a DNA molecule of another organism. DNA that contains pieces from different species is called **recombinant DNA**. It now has genetic material that is different from the original DNA pieces. When recombinant DNA is inserted back into the organism, it changes the organism's physical traits.

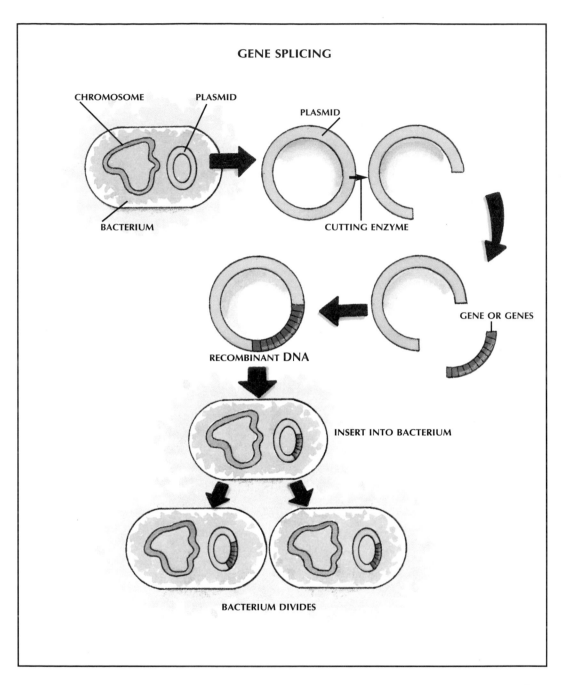

GENE SPLICING

CHROMOSOME   PLASMID

PLASMID

BACTERIUM

CUTTING ENZYME

GENE OR GENES

RECOMBINANT DNA

INSERT INTO BACTERIUM

BACTERIUM DIVIDES

In recombinant DNA work, scientists remove a plasmid from a bacterium, cut the plasmid open with restriction enzymes, and insert a gene that has been cut out using the same restriction enzymes. The plasmid is then put back into the bacterium, and special techniques are used to multiply the plasmid so that a single bacterium contains many copies of it. When the bacterium divides, it produces an exact copy of itself; each copy contains the plasmids, along with their inserted genes.

The recombinant DNA is then transplanted into a bacterium. Some bacteria have small rings of DNA, called **plasmids**, in addition to their chromosome. They typically code for traits such as resistance to antibiotics, and they are sometimes transferred from one bacterium to another. Researchers find plasmids useful as small "packages" for transferring and mass-producing genes.

These specially treated bacteria become little factories, producing large numbers of bacterial cells that contain the human gene. The "bacterial factories" provide a way to produce large amounts of proteins that normally occur in only tiny amounts. For example, researchers have used bacteria to produce human insulin, which is used to treat diabetes. Bacterial cells have also been used to produce the medicine needed to treat people with hemophilia.

✦ "PHARMING" ✦

Genetically engineered bacteria growing in huge tanks are only one source of useful biochemicals. In today's fast-growing biotechnology industry, genes for human proteins can also be inserted into farm animals such as sheep, cows, pigs, and goats. Often the genetic changes are designed so that the animals secrete the human proteins in their milk. The milk can be collected regularly without harming the animals, and the human proteins can easily be isolated from it. Since farm animals can thus be used to produce *pharm*aceuticals (drugs), this kind of genetic engineering is often referred to as "pharming."

Animals whose genome contains inserted genes from another species are called **transgenic** animals. Transgenic pigs are already being used to produce human insulin, and transgenic sheep are a source of human growth hormone and a protein used to treat a lung disease, emphysema. Genetic changes in cattle genes might produce reduced-fat milk or milk that is better for people who cannot digest the milk sugar, lactose.

In addition to serving as living factories for producing human proteins, animal "pharming" can also lead to better farm animals. Australian researchers, for example, have produced genetically modified sheep that grow more wool. A genetically engineered hormone has been developed to cause sheep to shed their fleece, al-

> DID YOU KNOW?
>
> Human proteins secreted in the milk of transgenic sheep are the main products of the Scottish company that produced Dolly, the cloned sheep. The experiments that led to Dolly were actually intended to develop a way of making multiple copies of transgenic sheep.

lowing sheep raisers to harvest the wool without having to shear the sheep. Another Australian research team is working on a gene-splicing method to protect sheep from flies that lay their eggs in sheep's skin. They have spliced a gene for a tobacco protein into the sheep's sweat glands, hoping that the toxic chemical it produces will kill off burrowing fly larvae.

Growth hormone genes from a variety of species, from fish to chickens, mice, and humans, have been inserted into trout, salmon, and other fish. With the extra growth hormone, the transgenic fish grow much faster. Genetically modified salmon, for example, grow twice as fast as usual and can be raised on fish farms, without having to spend part of their life in the ocean.

Medical researchers hope that transgenic pigs will provide a source of replacement tissues and organs for transplanting into humans. Usually, **xenotransplants** (*xeno*- means "foreign") are rejected by the body because various chemicals they contain are identified as foreign by the body's immune defenses. But scientists are attempting to "knock out" the gene for an enzyme that puts certain sugar molecules that are recognized as foreign on the surface of pig

Researchers have inserted the gene for a human milk protein, lactoferrin, into cattle. Cows with this gene produce milk that is closer to human milk than regular cow's milk and might make a better formula for feeding human babies.

cells, reducing the danger of rejection. They are also adding genes for proteins that will make the pig tissues more humanlike.

✦ GENE THERAPY ✦

Copies of human genes produced in bacteria can be supplied to human cells with defective or missing genes, so that the healthy genes will take over. This kind of treatment is known as **gene therapy**. Gene therapy is typically used to treat genetic disorders and diseases where no effective treatment is available.

Medical experts believe that gene therapy is a promising new approach. However, it has generated some controversy. During the 1990s, some patients undergoing gene therapy showed little or no improvement in their conditions. Then in September 1999, a gene therapy patient, eighteen-year-old Jesse Gelsinger, who was being treated for a genetic liver disease, died due to complications of the therapy.

Despite this tragedy, there have been some small successes. At Children's Hospital in Philadelphia, for example, gene therapy helped children with hemophilia to make a blood-clotting protein they lacked. French doctors reported promising tests of gene therapy for children with a rare genetic defect that disables the body's immune defenses against infectious diseases and cancer. In Boston, researchers have been working with heart disease patients. These patients suffered from chest pain due to clogged arteries that prevented enough nourishing blood from reaching the heart muscle. Injecting genes that cause new blood vessels to grow into the patients' hearts prompted the formation of new blood supply routes and relieved the patients' chest pains.

The most encouraging gene therapy results so far have been in the treatment of cancer. Many cancers are caused by damage to genes that regulate the way cells grow and multiply. Radiations, from the ultraviolet (UV) rays of the sun to "hard radiations" such as X rays and gamma rays, can cause such damage. Genes can also be damaged by **carcinogens**, cancer-causing chemicals such as those found in cigarette smoke, and by errors in copying DNA when cells divide. One important cancer-preventing gene is called p53. It normally works to detect problems in a cell; if a cell has become cancerous, p53 directs it to commit suicide. Researchers believe that defects in p53 are involved in as many as 50 to 75 percent of all cancers in humans. In gene therapy experiments, scientists have inserted copies of the p53 gene into viruses that were first stripped of their disease-causing parts. The viruses carrying p53 were then used to infect cancer patients with lung cancer or tumors of the head and neck. In many patients, the tumors stopped growing, shrank, or even disappeared. The gene therapy treatments tried so far have not helped everyone, and sometimes their effects were only temporary. But researchers hope to improve the treatments. They are also testing combinations of gene therapy with chemotherapy (drug treatments) and radiation therapy.

Our growing knowledge of DNA is expanding our ability to improve living conditions and to save lives.

GLOSSARY

alleles—different forms of the same gene; for example, one allele of the gene for eye color produces blue eyes, and another allele produces brown eyes.

amino acids—building blocks of proteins.

antisense—a segment of DNA (or RNA) with nucleotide "spelling" opposite to that of a working gene or portion of it; it is used to block the action of the gene.

carcinogen—a cancer-causing substance.

carrier—an organism with one allele of a recessive trait; the organism does not show the trait but can pass on the gene for it to offspring.

cell—the basic unit of life.

cell division—the process by which one cell divides into two.

chromosomes—tiny threadlike structures that carry DNA, found within the nucleus of a cell.

clone—a cell, cell product, or organism that contains genetic material identical to the original.

codon—a three-letter sequence of nucleotides in the messenger RNA chain that codes for a specific amino acid in the production of a protein molecule.

crossing over—the process by which maternal and paternal chromosomes exchange genetic material, creating new combinations of genes.

cytoplasm—the substance between the cell membrane and the nucleus (or the nuclear body in bacteria).

deletion—a type of mutation that occurs when there is a removal of one or more bases from the DNA chain.

DNA (deoxyribonucleic acid)—the substance that carries the hereditary instructions for making proteins.

dominant—referring to the form of a trait that appears even if the organism has only one copy of the gene for it.

electrophoresis—a technique that sorts DNA fragments by moving them at different speeds along a layer of gel under the influence of electric current.

enzyme—a special protein that helps make chemical reactions take place.

exon—a portion of a gene containing the code for assembling amino acids into a protein.

fertilization—the process by which egg and sperm nuclei join.

fetus—a developing human in the period from three months after conception to birth.

genes—chemical units that determine hereditary traits passed on from one generation of cells or organisms to the next.

gene-splicing—isolating a piece of DNA and joining it to a DNA molecule of another organism.

gene therapy—a kind of treatment in which copies of human genes produced in bacteria can be supplied to human cells with defective or missing genes, so that the healthy genes will take over.

genome—the total amount of DNA in an organism.

genotype—a combination of alleles that is responsible for a trait.

hybrid—a cell that forms as a result of joining cells from two different species.

insertion—a type of mutation that occurs when one or more bases are added to the DNA chain.

intron—a segment of DNA within a gene that does not code for protein production.

jumping genes—segments of DNA that can move from one position on the chromosome to another, or even to a different chromosome.

junk DNA—portions of DNA in the genome that do not code for proteins and have no apparent function.

linked traits—traits determined by genes that are close together on the same chromosome and thus are usually inherited together.

mitochondrion (*pl.* **mitochondria**)—energy-generating structures in cells.

mutation—a chemical change in a gene, which may produce a new trait that can be inherited.

nucleotide—a building block of DNA or RNA; it consists of a nitrogen base, a sugar, and a phosphate.

nucleus—the control center of a cell, which contains its hereditary instructions and is surrounded by a membrane separating it from the rest of its contents.

oncogene—a gene that causes cells to grow uncontrollably, resulting in cancer.

ovum (*pl.* **ova**)—a female sex cell (egg cell).

PCR (polymerase chain reaction)—a technique in which a special enzyme is used to copy a small segment of DNA over and over, giving the testers more material to work with.

phenotype—the visible characteristics of an organism.

plasmid—a strand or loop of DNA that exists independently of the chromosome in bacteria or yeasts.

recessive—referring to the form of a trait that does not appear unless the organism has inherited two copies of the gene for it, one from each parent.

recombinant DNA—DNA that contains pieces from different species.

replication—the process by which DNA reproduces itself.

restriction enzymes—chemical "scissors" that cut up DNA.

RFLPs (restriction fragment polymorphisms)—DNA fragments obtained when chromosomes are cut with restriction enzymes; when separated by electrophoresis they form a pattern that looks like a bar code.

ribosome—tiny spherical structure that is involved in manufacturing proteins.

RNA (ribonucleic acid)—a substance that is similar to DNA but has only one strand. Several types of RNA are involved in making proteins.

sexual reproduction—a form of reproduction in which a sperm from a male organism joins with an ovum from a female to produce a new individual. This individual has characteristics of both parents.

sperm—a male sex cell.

substitution—a type of mutation that occurs when a correct base is replaced by an incorrect one.

transgenic—an organism containing inserted genes from another species.

translocation—a type of mutation that occurs when a piece of a chromosome breaks off and then reattaches, not to where it belongs, but to some other chromosome.

xenotransplantation—transplanting cells, tissues, or organs from other species.

FURTHER INFORMATION

Books

Aldridge, Susan. *The Thread of Life: The Story of Genes and Genetic Engineering.* New York: Cambridge University Press, 1996.

Bauerle, Patrick, and Norbert Landa. *How the Y Makes the Guy.* Hauppauge, NY: Barron's, 1997.

————. *Ingenious Genes: Microexplorers.* Hauppauge, NY: Barron's, 1997.

Frank-Kamenetskii, Maxim D. *Unraveling DNA: The Most Important Molecule of Life.* Reading, MA: Perseus Books, 1997.

Gonick, Larry, and Mark Wheelis. *The Cartoon Guide to Genetics.* New York: HarperPerennial, 1991.

Goodsell, David S. *The Machinery of Life.* New York: Copernicus Books, 1998.

Jefferis, David. *Cloning: Frontiers of Genetic Engineering.* New York: Crabtree Publishing Company, 1999.

Pollack, Robert. *Signs of Life: The Language and Meanings of DNA.* New York: Houghton Mifflin Company, 1994.

Rensberger, Boyce. *Instant Biology: From Single Cells to Human Beings, and Beyond.* New York: Fawcett Columbine, 1996.

————. *Life Itself: Exploring the Realm of the Living Cell.* New York: Oxford University Press, 1996.

Tagliaferro, Linda, and Mark V. Bloom. *The Complete Idiot's Guide: Decoding Your Genes.* New York: Alpha Books, 1999.

Video

Nova—Cracking the Code of Life, WGBH Boston, 2001.

INTERNET RESOURCES

http://dna2z.com/DNA-o-gram "The DNA-o-gram Generator" (send someone an e-mail message in DNA code) and "DNA from A to Z" (zany uses of DNA).

http://gslc.genetics.utah.edu/ "Genetic Science Learning Center: Helping people understand how genetics affects our lives and society."

http://gwis2.circ.gwu.edu/~mcdonald/educ180/nih/DNA_tutorial.html "Hands On: DNA Fingerprinting," by Frank Hartel and Chanchai Singhanayok.

http://kidshealth.org/teen/health_problems/diseases/genes_genetic_disorders.html "The Basics on Genes and Genetic Disorders."

http://vector.cshl.org/ "Gene Almanac" (site of the DNA Learning Center at Cold Spring Harbor Laboratory; features include animations, audio, and video).

http://wire.ap.org/APpackages/genetic_engineering/gen-proto.html "Genetic Engineering Primer" (how genetic engineering works).

http://www.fbi.gov/hq/lab/org/dnau.htm "FBI Laboratory: DNA Analysis."

http://www.howstuffworks.com/link146.htm "An Animated Tutorial about the Basics of DNA, Genes, and Heredity," by Marshall Brain.

http://www.ornl.gov/TechResources/Human_Genome/home.html "Human Genome Project" (official Web site of the program).

http://www.pbs.org/wgbh/aso/tryit/dna/ "DNA Workshop: You Try It" (an interactive tutorial on DNA replication and protein synthesis).

http://www.sciencemag.org/feature/data/genomes/landmark.shl "Genome Landmarks" (February 16, 2001, issue of *Science)*.

http://www.thetech.org/exhibits_events/online/genome/ "DNA: the Instruction Manual for All Life" (information, activities—convert your name to a DNA alphabet, search for the sequence game—and ethical questions).

INDEX